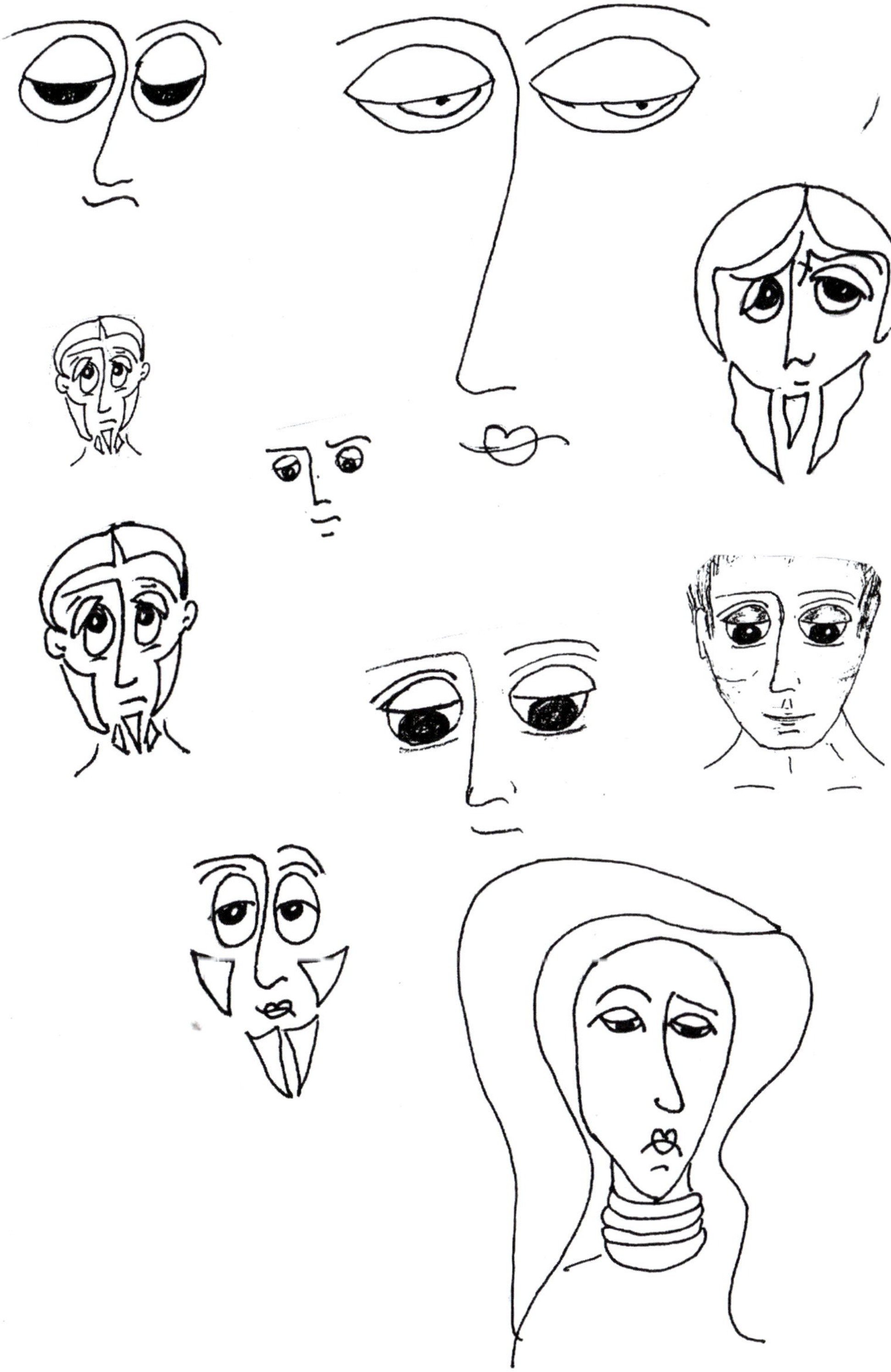

I would like to thank:

- Mother Teresa of Calcutta, and Mother Antonia, the prison angel, for their service and inspiration.
- The Sisters of the House of Loretto of Canton for wrapping their love around me and my girls
- Florence Hendrickson, my beloved spiritual mentor and friend, whose guidance I hear in my heart.
- Mary Bates, my professor and treasured friend, who turned me on to Southwest art and culture.
- My daughters Alicia McDonald, Falicia Burgess, and Brittney Burgess, and my grandson, Jake and his dad John Wesley Watson, for loving me in spite of myself.

ISBN# 978-0-9842976-3-4   v.1, 2.edition,softcover
1-4392-2476-5   v.1, 1.edition, softcover   978-1-4392-2476-2

Library of Congress Control Number 2010914626

Carol E. Briney, author and artist

Softcover printed in 2010 by Bookmasters, Inc., Ashland, OH, USA

Front cover painting by Carol E. Briney, retablo #41, St. Roy

Graphic Design and typography by Dan Szwedko

Contact Information:
Reentry Bridge Network, Inc., Publisher
408 Ninth Street SW
Canton, OH 44707
www.ReentryBridgeNetwork.org

Other books by Carol E. Briney:
Prison Coffee Table Book Project, Volume 1 and Volume 2

Sept. 13, 2015

David –
I love you.
Thanks for being my friend. Miss you.
Carol Brening

Dedicated to the individual men and women who honor me by participating in my workshops inside America's prisons

Table of Contents

NOTES AND QUOTES

affect, (af-fect'),

n., 1. A disposition or tendency. [Obs.] 2. in psychology, (a) an emotion, feeling, or mood as a factor in behavior; (b) a stimulus arousing an emotion, feeling, or mood. [It applies to individuals and their emotional epiphanies. The affect is the emotional impact that happens as a result of a spontaneous paradigm shift in thinking]
vt. To act upon; to move the feelings of; to aim at; to pretend.
Synonyms for affect are: to touch, to stir, to move.

Saint, n., by Carole Armstrong, Lives and Legends of the Saints:
"In the early days of Christianity, Paul used the term 'saints' to describe all his fellow Christians. Later, as more people were converted to the faith, the Church decided to award the title of "Saint" to martyrs – men or women who chose to die rather than renounce their faith – to miracle workers, and to the first monks, who gave up family life to serve Christ.

Saints in paintings are traditionally portrayed with halos – blazing circles of light around or behind their heads. Even when they are not named, they can often be identified by their symbols – objects or emblems connected with their lives or legends. Saint Michael, for example, holds a pair of scales to weigh the souls of men and women and Saint Lucy carried a pair of eyes on a handle or a plate.

While some of the saints in this book are remembered for their courageous lives and others for the legends woven around them, all have inspired the world's greatest artists to commemorate them gloriously in painting."

RETABLO HISTORY, by Larry Frank

"In northern New Mexico, once part of Mexico, and called New Spain, a unique and wondrous folk art evolved during the period of 1780-1907. This art was first introduced by settlers from Mexico who came to colonize a harsh and rugged land inhabited by Southwest Pueblo Indians. To satisfy their hunger for spiritual sustenance in this vast landlocked frontier, the colonists continued their tradition of creating santos, Catholic devotional images of saintly or angelic personages. Because of the extreme isolation of the folk artisans or santeros (saint makers) a distinctive and vigorous art was born whose style differed from mainstream Spanish Baroque imagery. Original and unorthodox, the New Mexican santos have a direct emotional appeal and appear completely uncluttered and naïve compared to their elaborate and realistic Spanish cousins.

Santos come in two forms, either retablos (painted wooden panels) or bultos (hand-carved three-dimensional wood sculptures.) Pine was used in making most of the retablos. Gesso was applied and the paints used were pigments derived from vegetables and minerals indigenous to the area. Each of the santeros who worked during the classic period, 1780-1907, such as Pedro Fresquis, the Laguna Santero; Molleno, the Santo Nino Santero; Jose Aragon and Rafael Aragon, carved and painted in his own individual style. The santeros were regarded by the villagers as master artists.

Santos adorned homes, chapels, churches, and moradas (penitente meeting places.) At birth, each new family member was assigned a saint as a namesake, friend, benefactor, and protector. The santos functioned as intercessors between humans and God and reigned supreme in New Mexican villages. Occupying the majority of Hispanic households as virtual members of the family, the saints held the keys to Divine power. Today, these remarkable images radiate the same vibrant immediacy and spiritual force that they did long ago. We can appreciate the vital niche that this rich cultural heritage has carried in the history of American art."

COMPOSITION OF MEDIUM

The traditional New Mexican retablos were painted on sugar pine planks. One coat of hot rabbit skin glue was first painted on to the wood to prepare it for the gesso layers. Gypsum or whiting was mixed with the remaining hot liquid rabbit skin glue to make the natural gesso. Several layers of gesso were then applied, reversing paint strokes with each layer, and thoroughly drying between coats. The gessoed plank was then sanded to the texture desired by the santero.

The traditional retablo pigments were extracted from plants, insects, and dirt; ingredients found in the environments of early pioneering Spanish settlers. The varnish was made from pinion tree sap nodules and alcohol. Note, if pinion sap is not available, do not substitute other tree sap as it may go on clear and later change to pink or brown, which is not desireable. Inside prisons, where alcohol is prohibited in any form, we simply rub a bar of beeswax onto the dry surface of the watercolor pigment retablos. A blow dryer will even out the wax, and a soft cloth will buff it out.

As a result of availability, economic feasibility, environmental impact, and desired intensity, I combined several medium scenarios. Each of the retablos in this book have their mediums documented.

MY RETABLO AWAKENING, March 1999

My introduction to the world of retablos came as a result of registering for a one-day workshop at a home studio in Chimayo, New Mexico. My decision to take that class was two fold: I desired to add another medium to my craft repertoire and I hoped it would generate an idea for handmade Christmas gifts. I had always been intrigued with the home shrines and popularity of saints within the Mexican culture of New Mexico. Having been reared Baptist and electing metaphysics as an adult, my exposure to "saints" had been very limited and opinionated; therefore, I felt that the class would give me insight. The trip would also take me to the mystical village of Chimayo and the day would, at the very least, prove to be fun and entertaining.

I was so anxious for the day, I left the house early and arrived in Chimayo, New Mexico, just as shops were beginning to open. I slowly perused a few and then drove through the village making mental notes on the wares of the tiny stores and artisans. I then stopped at the renown Santuario de Chimayo, and walked through the sanctuary with an air of indifference. I was not at all aware of the infamous back room. I checked my watch, and drove back down the road to the teacher's studio.

The workshop began at 10:00 a.m. and ended at 6:00 p.m. We were very busy all day. The teacher showed us the traditional way that the retablos were created in northern New Mexico, nearly 300 years ago. We learned about rabbit skin glue, homemade gesso, natural paint pigments, and my favorite: varnish made from pinion tree sap nodules. She had library books describing the lives of saints, and photo albums showcasing retablos and bultos painted by her and her children. With excitement, we students leafed through books and albums, seeking inspiration for the design and painting of our own retablo saint. We painted with ground-up cochineal bugs, dirt, and other natural plant pigments like pioneers had done for generations before us, adapting to their invironment in order to create their beloved santos images and paintings.

At noon, we drove down to the Santuario de Chimayo to eat lunch in the courtyard and to see the historical retablos, reredos and bultos. We also hoped to visit the back room where a hole in the wooden floor reveals the holy dirt beneath it. The legend of this ancient adobe mission church is that the holy dirt from the replenishing hole in the floor can bring about miraculous healings and the long pilgrimages that hundreds of people make to the church each Easter. As we entered the crowded little room where crutches and other artifacts, left behind by recipients of the healing miracles of the holy dirt, covered the walls, my eyes went to a young boy who was prayerfully kneeling down and gathering holy dirt for his grandmother. I gingerly asked him if he would also scoop a small amount for me. I wrapped the dirt up in one of the brochures I had gotten from the lobby of the church. I collected the holy dirt because, at that time, I thought it would add a nice touch to my future retablo paintings. My knee and leg would not allow me to bend down and gather the dirt myself. In fact, I was not even able to respectfully kneel at the alter as I passed through the sanctuary. I now found myself bothered by my physical inabilities to respect the ancient rituals of the mission which our teacher had spoken of, and I felt at a loss that I was so closed and unfamiliar with Catholic teachings that I did not really know how to enter into the emotional and mental reverence that I felt was respectful of my surroundings. I felt awkward and intrigued.

There were two other ladies in the class with me. They were both Catholic and had studied Russian Orthodox iconography and Mexican retablos. This was not a new medium or subject for them. They were taking the class especially to study with our teacher. I was not yet aware of exactly who she was in the retablo arena.

When it came time to decide which saint we would paint, it came to me through a likeness in one of the books illustrating saints, that I would not only enjoy painting a retablo of Swami G., with whom I had recently studied, but I would also enjoy having his likeness hanging in my home. So, I began sketching. The picture seemed to develop itself with ease, as I have found with all of my retablos. I really felt that I had outdone myself. Never before had I been able to draw people, yet I felt Swami G and my two girls were perfect (This was, in fact, the beginning of my art career.)

I was the only student to finish my retablo and I was totally high from the entire day's experience. I was also the only one to paint a "non-Catholic," "non-saint" subject. As a result, I had yet another twinge of discomfort in my process. But, most importantly, I left class with a finished retablo that meant a great deal to me. I cherished it and could hardly wait to get home and hang my Swami G retablo on our living room wall.

The trip back to Albuquerque was roughly two hours of silence in a car with a broken radio. My never-quieted, forever-analytical mind wasted no time delving into the examination of this retablo process and who the subjects have traditionally been. I examined what life must have been to these individuals prior to sainthood. I examined the attachment that Catholicism places on the influence of the dead upon the living. I examined the fact that in the Protestant culture, the retablos were and are considered idolatrous sacrilegious pagan objects revered by Catholics. When, in fact, the retablos were cherished storyboards for an illiterate society, and for teaching the children. They were also an affordable decoration that came with blessings and meaning to a poor culture. They were a symbol of hope and strength in a life of struggle and would-be hopelessness. They were a reminder of God's presence in the lives of humanity.

Well into my journey home, I examined what I had personally learned and experienced and began formulating how my new knowledge could be applied towards Christmas presents. How could I apply this and come up with presents suitable for a family of Texas Baptists and Methodists? I had to laugh at the assignment I had given myself and proceeded to turn on my backdoor creative juices. I began exploring my multi-faceted perspective.

I also was giving thought to the fact that I had just painted a living person who had brought a lot of spiritual awakening and good into my life. This person was not Catholic nor did he fit the criteria of sainthood according to Roman stipulations. So, I asked myself to whom else do I look for Divine inspiration and knowledge? Whose image would I like to have in my home shrine, or sitting on my altar? Whose teachings do my collections of artifacts represent? I found my list to be easy and the thought of experiencing the process of painting each of them as a retablo was very exhilarating to me.

From that thought, I returned to Christmas. With Christmas comes handmade gifts to my family and friends. In my mind's eye, I began examining each person on my list, and I had the epiphany of painting my family members as saints. Well, I don't have to tell you that that thought comes with a jolt and a personal checkup. The first vision comes with sneaking little symbols of judgment of their character into the drawing in such fashion they'd never really know I had slipped it in, and giggled while doing it. But I'd know the small victory, and felt shame for inserting those thoughts into my mental process. I then visualized seeing each of them from inside their own head and heart, and began seeing them through the eyes of their best friends, their children, and their spouse. Those visualizations, those persons were entirely different than the family members I had always had in my personal "story." Wake-up call! I began to wonder what I had missed that others had seen. How much of my own emotions and story had I transferred or just flat out piled onto my perception of these people? These people were made by God, with a purpose, and placed in my life to be part of my purposeful journey. I clearly recognized that I needed to get through the garbage to the God and see the magic of the souls that stand before me, walk beside me, and support my Goodness, even if it appears to just not be that way. I remembered the lessons of duality. I realized I could use this process to see clearly. It is that moment of awareness: of "got it." It is that quantum spark that moves the soul in such a way that it effects our entire life. That split second emotional epiphany is called the affect. What follows is the effect.

Then came the thump on the head from my own personal core belief that we are all spiritual Christs made entirely of God. That we are God experiencing, and this One Reality also includes all of the family and friends on my Christmas list. The friends are easy. They are in my life as I have chosen. The family, that's not so easy. That's a bundle of unfinished business and judgment. That's just not a very comfortable place to throw ones thoughts into, especially when you make yourself stay there and think about it. I asked myself why is it that the people who are on our Christmas list are the ones we have the most issues with and yet we maintain our attachment to them? Is this not evidence that we have somehow chosen these individuals and we are depending on one another to journey through this life of learning? I stayed in that thought for a minute and then resurfaced.

I took the hardest reframe and began with him. Most of the people who live in my head didn't want to participate in the assigned project and left. The more saintly of the group began with the fact of Goodness. Layer after layer of garbage and goop was peeled back until I stood in view of only Goodness in this individual. Speechless and even ashamed, I walked the corridors of my head and heart. Again. Then I began to draw in my mind's eye a vision of how I would paint that individual as a saint. What attributes describe his life essence? What symbols could I use to reflect those attributes? Why was he in my life, and what was his life about, truly? As my ego stepped out of the way, I realized I had missed some gifts some meaningful conversations and experiences that had been available to me.

As I continued down the road home, in the quiet darkness of highway and me, and all those people who argue inside my head, I started feeling guilty that I had not paid due homage to traditional saints and retablos. I had this feeling that perhaps by painting Swami G, I was sacrilegious and disrespectful in our teacher's culture in her own home. I committed to paint at least one traditional saint, for penitence and pure experience.

My thoughts returned to family and friends. Or just family. My mind fluttered from individual to individual, assessing and painting through my list then the profound question came: *What would I look like if THEY painted ME as a saint?* How much trouble would they have with that concept? And then further into the self-examination: *How would I paint ME as a saint? What would my depiction be? What are my attributes? What does my life stand for?*

Well, anyone who knows me very well, knows that by this point in the process, my mind is creating a full experience and a workshop is being born to explain and share with others. My passion gets turned on and I get obsessed with the journey of and through the process. I was pumped!

What if a group came together and learned the traditional retablo and reredo process (reredo is a connected grouping of more than one retablo) and the first saint they painted was up to them, like my first one was of Swami G.

The students would spend all day Saturday learning technique and painting their first retablo of choice and inspiration. Their homework assignment as class breaks up is to pick an individual in their life that they talk negatively about or have ill feelings toward and peel away the layers until they come to the Christ, the Goodness that this individual brings to life and to be ready to visualize and design that individual as a saint. They would be directed to come to class the next Saturday ready to paint this retablo. In fact, a student could commit to choose 12 such individuals and paint one each month of the year. What if at Christmas you presented those individuals with the gift of themselves as a retablo santos and a brief description of their sainthood penciled on the back of the wooden panel? How powerful would that be? The exchange of Goodness and the reframing would be extremely profound and life changing.

The third assignment would be to paint a traditional saint. The presence of numerous santos books through which to leaf would make the inspiration easy. Perhaps even tour some of the old village Catholic churches in New Mexico to see and experience the reredos first hand, even if it is done virtually online. The students could even make sketches as they viewed the reredos while sitting in contemplation. If the student had done this with the first retablo, then instruct them to paint a living saint, or one who has died more recently, even if not yet canonized.

I think that the fourth retablo should be a self portrait. The fifth retablo should be of God.

One of the "ah-ha" experiences I had when I was trying to design my family reredo, was that, as I read through the saint books from the library, observing technique and stories, I realized that I knew at least one person that fit the description of virtually every one of the saints that I read about. The parallels were astounding. I realized that I could paint traditional saints and tweak them ever so slightly to represent family and others. It amazed me as I pondered the history of seeing the Good in people and then capturing the revelation as a painting. As a culmination of all of this thought, I chose four traditional saints to represent my four family members and painted them as a reredo family portrait.

After this mental exercise, I have found that I tend to view everyone differently than before. Upon meeting them, my mind begins reframing and designing a retablo of them. Often it is a laborious process. Sometimes, I must confess, the warrior in me is quicker to draw my sword than to find my way back to the questions of who and why. Especially around the individuals who I perceive threaten the ones I choose to guard. It doesn't always come easy for me to reframe, or to be conscious that I should follow my own teachings. However, words usually find their way to my ears, head, and heart, and I try to eliminate the garbage and see the God, the Goodness, the saint, and unwrap the present before me, realizing that duality is the teacher. This is not always an easy thing to do, but the thought, the concept, never leaves me.

I can honestly say that I have now participated in and conquered many art media with success and validation. However, none of them have bonded with my soul as this has. I am compelled and obsessed with this expression of God. I doodle retablo faces and bodies, always looking for new simple lines to capture emotion. I have found this process to be very therapeutic, enlightening, and inspirational. I have also found that my creative skills and talents are more focused and finely tuned. And, I do, in fact, fall in love with each and every one of my retablos and it is a struggle to part with them. You can often find me with pen in hand, doodling on napkins and explaining to anyone who will listen, how modest stick figures can change the course of a life.

One of the great things about painting retablos is that you don't have to be a master artist to successfully create a retablo. The most famous retablos in New Mexico's history look like a six year old child painted them. You can't not succeed. Retablos are simple folk art storyboards. I have a tendency to complicate mine with details, but then again, one of life's lessons that I continually chase is that of finding simplicity in all that I do. In anything that I do.

I truly believe that an individual cannot sit down and paint a retablo without being connected to the individuals reflected in the retablo. I have experienced this each and every time that I have painted. I have also used the process as a means of communicating and visiting with old friends as I talk through the day's problems, or thank them, or forgive them or myself. The individuals do not have to be dead or out of your life for this process to work.

I have had many phenomena occur with the paintings, in the paintings, and as a result of the paintings. Faces, symbols, and imagery show up in the watercolors sometimes days and weeks after completion; sometimes within hours. The images come and go with time. For a long while, I shared that observation with only a few close friends. Now, I recognize all of it as part of the process.

The week following my class was Holy Week, or Easter. In New Mexico, a predominantly Catholic culture, Good Friday is observed as much or more than Easter. I decided to spend Friday through Sunday in great thought and ceremony, or ritual. I was not physically able to join the long holy walk from Albuquerque to Chimayo or to Belen's Tome Hill, so, I decided I would paint myself there in spirit. On Friday night, I began by painting a retablo of a young girl, her father and a friend carrying crosses as they made the long pilgrimage to Chimayo. Saturday night, I painted a young man as Christ, carrying a life-size cross up Tome Hill. I challenged my daughter, Alicia, to paint the anguish of Mary, as a human mother, on that actual Saturday night of the crucifixion. Since I did not find a representation of the resurrection in my retablo books, I decided to paint a happy, but perceptive, young Mary and Jesus on Easter Sunday. It was in that search through the library books that I became aware that the Catholic culture focused on the crucifixion and the Protestants, on the resurrection. I found the weekend to be very enlightening and meaningful.

Ever since I took the class, I felt guilt about our teacher's possible feelings of sacrilege towards my painting a retablo of a non-Catholic figure. I had read some separateness into our three brief phone conversations since class. Then I received a phone call from her on April 24. She shared with me that the day after our workshop, her daughter had given premature birth to twins who had lived only one day and made their transition back to God. She had been with the beloved twins from beginning to end, wrapping them in love and prayers. What I heard in her voice was a sorrow and mourning that she had not yet been ready to share. As she told me of the extreme heartache that this loss had brought to her and the family, she told me that she had never before painted anyone other than Catholic saints because she considered it to be sacrilege. But when the twins died, she thought of me, and she told me that she had painted the twins as saints; after all they had come directly from God, and were indeed little saints.

This process is powerful and the subtle and profound ripples are many. I am again reminded that you never know who you touch from moment to moment in this life. You never really know whose life you change.

As I have canvassed individuals regarding this process, I have posed the question: *If you were to die and I were to paint you as a saint, what attributes would your life reflect?* I find that the majority of the young people are quick to answer based on who they dream of being and what they want and hope to give to the world. We older people have a tendency to roll our eyes, cock our head and begin to search our hearts and mind for the residue that we might leave behind. The answer is most commonly: "I don't know. I hope that I've done something that mattered."

It's a heavy question and a loaded answer. But the good side of the process is that we most likely will become what we paint ourselves to be, no matter what age we pick up the brush. It is, after all, our canvas, our paint, and our brush.

REFLECTIONS - September 15, 1999

I have now completed 38 paintings and feel compelled to reflect on what exactly has happened to me through this process, this journey.

Last night, I identified ten scenarios that had generated these first 38 retablo paintings. At this time, I feel it is important to explore in more detail why each of these categories arose in my life; what my psyche was hoping to gain through the process; what exactly occured as a result of my spending hours of intense visual expression in each sitting; what golden threads run through this human life to avail such a patterning; and why are the affects of the process so impregnated into the heart and mind that such resolve is definite upon completion of each painting. Why is the impact of the finished retablo so personal and so animated that I awake in the night and walk through the house to be in the presence of them, checking over and over to reaffirm that the results and God energy are still there reminding and assuring me that "I am." What connects me so strongly to these simple planks? Who are the entities veering back from the other side of the pigments? What is it exactly that I must glean from the affects of the retablo process and present to others around me? Where am I going with this, and where exactly is it that I have been? What forces drive me to obsess with these simple paintings?

In the essence of order, I shall look at each of the ten categories individually and assess the needs and the benefits as they appear to me today. And, of course, I rightfully expect that this will change as I grow. According to Ralph Waldo Emerson, this is okay.

Having been reared in a Protestant environment and strongly warned against eternal damnation for paganism and blasphemy, I had not ever acquainted myself with any of the traditional Catholic saints other than those who blatantly crossed my path enough to be remembered by name only: Mary, St. Francis, St. Christopher, Michael the Archangel. It was my conditioning that the only acceptable religious paintings were the generic ones such as happy Jesus, winged guardian angels helping children across bridges, and the last supper. Therefore, as I sat down on the sofa to flip through the five picturesque saint books

I checked out from the local library, I did, in fact, deal with a bit of a tinge of Baptistism. But, as I read through the books, I again became captivated in the parallels that I found. Saint after saint reminded me of someone who had brought cherished values into my life. Such an epiphany that the same characters have evolved throughout each century of this human timing, even by generation, and here were my friends and gurus as painted by the great masters of Europe and New Mexico.

With that realization, I plunged into the perspective of observing these people from the human element. What went on in their real lives? Who were their friends? What were their personal processes and ordeals? How did they refine relationships? How did they define God? What was their personal relationship to their God? What was myth? What was down-to-earth life like for them? What was their point of reference? I sat for hours through the night attempting to meet these people on a human level, conversing with them in my mind's eye. What did the artist St. Luke paint? How did Joan of Arc tap into such wisdom, warrior strength, and charisma at the age of 14? What was a day like in the hermit life of John the Baptist, living to himself as the animals in the jungle, yet talking only of God? What was the human relationship of Mary Magdalene and Jesus? How did she emotionally survive Jesus' death and his ascension? What fear and feeling of abandonment must have been like for Peter that lead him to deny Jesus thrice, and his penitence and sorrow that followed the disappointments he had of himself? St. George the dragon slayer was chosen to represent chivalry and triumph over good and evil. So does this verify the existence of dragons, or was everything about him a mythological story created to inspire the crusading soldiers? Was St. Francis of Assisi the first saint noted to telepathically communicate with the animals and plants? Obviously he was the most noted environmentalist. What exactly did he tell them? St. Christopher was a third-century giant who worked as a ferryman, carrying travelers across a deep river. Obviously his life was hard, dirty, isolated, and monotonous. Why was he chosen to bear the Christ child across the river, as the weight of the world? And Joseph. Such subtle strength and wisdom. The perfect father and friend figure to raise a perfect son. What thoughts were in his mind and heart? What of him at the crucifixion? No one ever speaks of his sorrow and weeping over his son. How did Mary survive the night of the crucifixion of her perfect and loving son? Even she obviously had doubts about Jesus' resurrection. How did she feel when she saw him and knew she had doubted him, and that he was ascending? Was the brown-skinned Virgin of Guadalupe created for the Spaniards to convert the Native American Indians to Catholicism? Which saints were authentic and which were created to validate excessive laws of man and strict, literal translations of the Bible? Which were examples of archetypical lives, or just political ploys to control populaces? Which were merely exaggerations of real lives, grown through unwritten legends? Which were literal, though bazaar? How many kings and Caesars controlled nations through Catholic saints? Or, are we to embrace the history of every documented saint at face value, without questions?

The questions and parallels go on and on. The speculation as to what the true story was and which saints were created by authority in order to establish political gain and law, is endless. And the fact is that it does not matter at all. It is the intent of establishing God-unity that is underlying in all of the stories.

As I spent the past several weeks pondering these questions, trying to match them with answers, I also began to examine the tradition of assigning a favored saint to guard over a

child's entire life, even from birth. What affect does this bear on a personality?
From that thought, my mind connected to one of my original exercises with retablos: That of asking everyone, "If I painted you as a saint, what attributes would you have?" As I formerly stated, the teens through mid-twenties answer rather readily. We older citizens usually roll our eyes in an attempt to locate the remains we've left behind. But, what of the young toddlers and adolescents that are just doing what's in front of them at the time? Living life as it opens up to them. Who are they and what characteristics are they already naturally demonstrating? If I were to paint them as the saint I feel most parallels them, and then spend their life telling them of this, what affect would there be on that life? I recall the infamous architect, Frank Lloyd Wright, and the history of his mother doing just that, except it centered around his becoming the greatest architect who ever lived.

I have, at the time of this writing, spent some six months intensely and wholly involved in this examination. I find it to be a subtle and powerful chameleon in the full circle of life. From this narrative, I hope it is easy to see how I organized my thoughts to paint friends, relatives, gurus and spiritual mentors as retablos. The process that I described of getting through the garbage and seeing the God in people is what is called reframing.

There were events that impacted my life in such a way that I desired to capture them in a retablo. I could have also used an ex voto, which is a retablo story board with text. And there were holidays and anniversaries that I chose to do ritual or ceremony by capturing the emotions, whatever they might be, in the essence of a retablo.

When I am asked to paint a retablo as a gift to a third party, I use the descriptors given to me by the patron to plug into the essence of the individual's life and try to capture who that person is through the patron's eyes.

Perhaps the most profound of all scenarios, is that of capturing the peak of a relationship as a retablo. As humans, when we get into a romantic relationship, it is all positive and rosy at the beginning. We tell our friends how wonderful the person is, and we spend hours wondering if "this is the one"? We brag about their attributes to our friends and family. And then when it all starts to fall apart, because they "aren't the one", we humans tend to begin destroying the person we were previously so excited about. We seem to feel that we can't leave a relationship until we have destroyed the other person. Somehow it justifies our leaving. Or their leaving. Why can't we just say, "it was great, but we both have other interests and are just going to remain friends?" By painting a retablo that is all about the peak of the relationship, all of the goodness that attracted you into it, and kept you in the relationship, you are able to hold onto it and its best memories. You are then actually moving from destruction to celebration. The retablos that I painted of past relationships are nearest and dearest to me. They make me smile and feel the hugs.

The hardest retablo to paint is the one of self. You will need input from trusted friends who understand your questions. Sometimes a mere acquaintance will have a clearer perception of who you are. An immense amount of reflection is required to see oneself in ones story without the negative self talk and denial.

Then there's the capturing of God's essence as a retablo. That one doesn't come easily either. Lots of theology and physics. This is a very personal retablo that no one but you will know when it is right. It's a fun and challenging project to undertake. For some, the process lies in defining and refining one's own thoughts. For others, the process requires the reframing process I described in my Awakening chapter. In all scenarios, one has to set ego and judgment aside and feel purpose and patterns within.

Though I strongly feel it is undeniable that dastardly deeds have taken place and nations have been controlled in the name of God and saints, with my heart in hand, I again place before you the truth of your being and every other person in this human experience, as I believe it to be. We are all great big Divine spirits trying very hard to have a little bitty human being experience in this lifetime. We are created by and out of God. God is all there is, ever has been, or ever will be. Omnipresent. Omnipotent. Omniscient. Alpha and Omega. It is impossible to separate us from God. Every human being is to be observed from your heart to theirs. Cut through the garbage and find the saint, the spirit, the Christ, the Love, God, the One Reality. Open the presents before you. That is what I believe and is the point from which I paint.

NINE YEARS LATER – October 2008

It's been nine years since I began this book manuscript. I had tucked it away in a file cabinet when I began pursuing my college education. Next week I will celebrate my 61st birthday and I proudly share with you that I have earned my Associates of Arts, Liberal Arts degree from Central New Mexico Community College; my Bachelor of Arts, Fine Arts degree, with a minor in psychology, from the University of New Mexico; and am currently a Liberal Studies graduate student at Kent State University here in Ohio. My multi-discipline graduate program is titled Reducing Recidivism in the Prison Community. I am also the executive director of The Prison Coffee Table Book Project, a national non-profit organization that brings the art muses into prisons as a means of self-expression, healing and growth, in addition to publishing the art and writings of individuals who are incarcerated across America. The programs and projects are many, therefore I shall leave the description brief.

You may ask: "How does all of that tie into this manuscript?" My answer would be "Perfectly." For you see, it was the epiphany of the retablo affect that took me to college at the age of 50. It is the message of the retablo effect that I carry into prisons so that those individuals can have tools through which they can reframe the community around them. And most importantly, so they can truly see themselves. In addition, the art of retablos is such that anyone can draw or paint the images. I certainly had no formal art training in 1999. I'd never painted a human image before Swami G. This art form gives the inmates permission to express themselves through a simple and primitive art medium. To capture and work through emotions. To heal and grow. Whether it is remorse or reverence, the retablo affect gives them tools and opens their world to a different dimension.

Though the manuscript has been safely tucked away, I have presented the lecture many times in churches, prisons, and on speaking engagements. It was the prisoners, however, who asked me if I would facilitate a hands-on retablo workshop and teach them to paint themselves as a retablo. That request was most profound for me. Those eight hours, spent with 50 incarcerated individuals are so intensely emotional and intimate with sharing that they carve indelible images on my heart. I get how important this work is. I get how important it is that I finish this manuscript and have it as a footprint that goes beyond my capabilities.

So, I have chosen to use the texts that I wrote in 1999, updating where needed, in an attempt to keep the story and the awakening fresh. During these nine years, I have expanded my retablo images to collages, found art assemblages and shrines, and found art bultos. I must confess that more of my time is spent in writing of the phenomena of the arts than in producing them. However, I have just picked up my watercolor brush to add two more retablos to this compilation: my self-portrait ex voto, and Roy Dunlap, my cousin. It has taken these years to discover who I am and the purpose I evoke. In retrospect, it is easy for me to see that my entire life has been spent in training and grooming for my purpose of working with individuals who are incarcerated in America's prisons. I have not the least bit of doubt about that, and The Retablo Affect is the foundation for that work.

CHRIST IN AND AMONG US, St. Matthew, Chapter 25, Bible, King James Version

35. For I was an hungred, and ye gave me meat: I was thirsty, and ye gave me drink: I was a stranger, and ye took me in:

36. Naked, and ye clothed me: I was sick, and ye visited me: I was in prison, and ye came unto me.

40. And the King shall answer and say unto them, Verily I say unto you, Inasmuch as ye have done it unto one of the least of these my brethren, ye have done it unto me.

TEN RETABLO CATAGORIES

Traditional Retablo Saints
Living Saints
Events
Third Party Channel
Self
Gurus – Spiritual Mentors
Reframe
Relationship Processing
God (Note: I have decided not to include my painting of God because I do not want to lead or suggest an image to anyone who might set that as one of their painting goals.)

PAINTED ORDER: 1
RETABLO : Swami G - Guru/Spiritual Mentor
INSPIRATION: His Holiness Shri Swami Divyananda Saraswatiji Maharaj, better known as Reverend Guruji
MEDIUM: Natural pigment and water color, rabbit skin glue gesso, pinion sap varnish, bees wax, gouged pine plank, 7.5" x 12"
DESCRIPTION: I had recently attended several public lectures by Swami Guruji and was very enlightened and inspired by his teachings. He is an 85 year-old nonsectarian Swami who was imprisoned with Mahat Maghandi. After Maghandi's death, Swami G retreated to a cave at 17,000 feet in the snowy Himalayan Mountains, where he meditated for 40 years before his journey around the world to share what he has learned. He is also the founder of InterPeace.

As I leafed through the books of saints at our teacher's studio, I came upon a picture of St. William that reminded me of Swami G. I instantly envisioned him standing on the platform of my church, holding one finger up and saying, "There is only One Truth, and that is God. There is only One Lesson and that is Love. There is only One Reality and that is God. God is Goodness and Simplicity." I could see my two granddaughters, Brittney with her baby doll and Falicia, standing in front of him, the round light box of NASA's photo of Earth encircling his head as a halo from behind, and the candle stand beside him.

I added the fountain symbol in the lower left hand corner, the green ivy vines of Life in the top corners and down the sides, and developed the Religious Science emblem into the Himalayan Mountains in the top segment of the retablo.

This retablo hangs in my personal shrine so Swami G's words come to me every time my eyes look upon it.

It was not until 1:30 a.m. on Saturday preceding Easter Sunday that I noticed very obvious faces that are located in the blue and white NASA circle behind Swami G in this retablo. The powerful masculine face is one of my favorite things about this retablo. He looks so wise and strong to me: Godlike.

I had just finished my third retablo and was in the process of hanging it up when my peripheral vision noticed the faces. I almost whip lashed my neck. Coincidence? I laughed and thought, well, it will make a nice story…entities appearing in my retablos.

Swami G - Guru/Spiritual Mentor

PAINTED ORDER: 2
RETABLO: Celtic Cross - Ritual
INSPIRATION: Favored pair of earrings and my Irish heritage
MEDIUM: Natural pigment and water color, pure gypsum and rabbit glue gesso, sugar pine plank, 7.5" x 12", natural varnish
DESCRIPTION: Having just completed my retablo course with my teacher, I was looking for something easy and obvious to paint. I had spent the week gathering my supplies and chose a Celtic cross earring as my symbol pattern. The other symbols are African.

Since Albuquerque, New Mexico, has a gypsum mine, I used pure gypsum to mix my gesso. This is the only one of my retablos that has that base. The natural gypsum was too hot and therefore was very difficult to work with and not recommended. Obviously the original retablo artists used raw gypsum, and rabbit skin glue, however, I do not know the additional ingredient or process that they used to cool the gypsum so it would permanently adhere to the plank and maintain a smooth surface. This book includes the gesso recipe that my teacher instructed us to mix and use.

This retablo is a nice collection piece due to the emblem, significance of the many symbols, and the antique appearance.

Celtic Cross - Ritual

PAINTED ORDER: 3
RETABLO: St. Patrick - Guru/Spiritual Mentor
INSPIRATION: My pastor, Rev. Patrick
MEDIUM: Natural pigment and water color, rabbit skin glue gesso, sugar pine plank, 7.5" x 12", natural varnish
DESCRIPTION: Still unsure of what direction to go with my retablo subjects and designs, I chose my pastor as my subject. Patrick was a continual inspiration and strong spiritual leader and friend in my life, so the choice to create a retablo of him for my personal shrine was a definite.

Being a contemporary, surrealistic, symbolic type of artist who never had the knack for drawing or painting faces, I laid out my design so that it would make a symbolic, moving statement without having to paint faces.

I turned the Religious Science symbol upside down and created a mountaintop through a rainbow. I depicted Patrick leading the people up the mountain. The mountain also holds the voice of Martin Luther King, Jr. Patrick holds the tarot sword of intelligence and spirit in his left receiving hand, and the tarot cup of love in his giving right hand. Patrick wears a crown on his head that signifies that he realizes the Christ in himself and is robed in royal purple and red. All of the people, robed in green for Life, with varying skin tones, have halos and are positioned following Patrick up the mountain. There were two definite faces that later appeared in the sky, one on either side of the mountaintop

At this point of painting, I had not realized the seriousness of my new interest. I was still looking for the ins and outs of my creations. I was still busy trying to make a profound statement, instead of letting the statement make me, profoundly.

St. Patrick - Guru/Spiritual Mentor

PAINTED ORDER: 4
RETABLO: Chimayo Pilgrimage - Ritual/Celebration
INSPIRATION: Newspaper Photo
MEDIUM: Natural pigment, dirt, and water color, gesso, sugar pine plank, 7.5" x 12", natural varnish
DESCRIPTION: This retablo was the first in a series of three that I did over the 1999 Easter weekend. I could not walk the Chimayo pilgrimage or even the Tome Hill pilgrimage. Therefore, I made the commitment to participate in spirit through my paintbrush. I began Good Friday night by capturing a newspaper photo from the 1998 pilgrimage of a young girl, her father, and friend carrying crosses to Chimayo, New Mexico.

This was the first retablo to have dirt as one of the color pigments. I reasoned that since they were walking to the Santuario de Chimayo that I should use some of the Chimayo sacred dirt beneath their feet. I painted the top frame arch with the dirt my daughter, Alicia, had brought back from her Texas trip the previous week. I stepped the young girl onto the bottom frame for a three-dimensional effect.

It was this Easter weekend ritual that began my habit of painting a retablo through the night, totally unaware of time, and yet, being more rested the next morning than my full night's sleep would have left me. The average painting time is from 8:30 p.m. until 2:30 p.m. I have had to space myself to where I sleep at least every other night.

I had made the statement to my friend, Trish, that I did not see additional faces in this retablo. She quickly pointed out to me that the father, on the right side, had a profile of another face within his face. She said she felt that perhaps that was his counter person. Oddly enough, it was his face that looked off-center and peculiar to me. However, every time faces show up, they are located in the areas of the paintings that I have struggled with and given up on "fixing."

It was my success with this retablo that really launched my confidence and spirit into my retablo painting on all dimensions.

Chimayo Pilgrimage - Ritual/Celebration

PAINTED ORDER: 5
RETABLO: Tome Hill - Ritual/Celebration
INSPIRATION: Newspaper photo
MEDIUM: Natural pigment, dirt, and water color, gesso, sugar pine plank, 7.5" x 12", natural varnish
DESCRIPTION: I had chosen another newspaper photo to capture as my Saturday night retablo, as the second night of my Easter weekend spiritual ritual. This photo was of a young man bearing the weight of a life-size cross up Tome Hill, outside Belen, New Mexico.

I kept the same posture, however, I clothed the young man as Jesus, added both Marys to the crowd just in front of him, and painted the entire mountain with dirt from my daughter's trip home from Texas. As a last thought, I added Chimayo dirt to the area Jesus had already walked upon, due to its revered holiness.

About a month after I had finished this retablo, I carried it down to Kinko's to get color copies made of it. When they handed me the copies for approval of the color, I noticed there was a yellowing in the lower left quadrant of the copies. I was in a hurry, and didn't even focus or discuss it at that time. Late that night, my daughter was talking on the phone, sitting across the room from where the retablo was hanging. When she hung up the phone, she told me to come sit in the chair and look at it. The yellowing was an obvious angel facing Jesus. This, along with the many faces that have emerged from the Chimayo dirt pigment, make this one of the most intriguing of my collection. It is always the crowd favorite.

Tome Hill - Ritual/Celebration

PAINTED ORDER: 6
RETABLO: Virgin and Child - Ritual/Celebration/Traditional
INSPIRATION: The Human Thoughts of Mary
MEDIUM: Natural pigment, dirt, and water color, gesso, sugar pine plank, 7.5" x 12", natural varnish
DESCRIPTION: As I continued through my seventy-two hour ritual, I decided that I needed a happy subject for my Easter Sunday retablo. I searched through the library books and found not one retablo that depicted the resurrection. Because I wanted to utilize authentic New Mexican depiction, I did not design one of my own at this time. Therefore, trying to visualize some of Mary "the human mother's" thoughts on that day, I decided to paint the young Mother with her baby Son and how she must have held those unmarred memories ever so tightly in her heart that morning.

I used dirt for the adobe building behind them, with a yellow, lighted arch to serve as Mary's halo effect. The frame is also painted with dirt. I incorporated the Religious Science symbol into the rafters of the building along with two cherubs and a gathering of roses. The fountain and candlestick were symbols depicting light and life.

There are a few points of interest in this retablo. The heart with a sword in it at the bottom left corner symbolizes Mary's heartache to come. Mary's eyes and face tell you of her foreknowledge of the future events. There are numerous full-body entities and faces in this retablo. The most obvious is the large head in front of the fountain that appears to be blowing air at the candlestick and the gathering of people behind it. There is also a gathering of full-body people behind the fountain. Again, the green area was the area that I struggled to try to get a smooth pigment in and finally gave up on it, thinking I had overworked it and ruined it.

Virgin and Child - Ritual/Celebration/Traditional

PAINTED ORDER: 7
RETABLO: Lady of Sorrow - Ritual/Celebration
INSPIRATION: I asked Alicia to paint the retablo as Easter ritual
MEDIUM: Water color, gesso, sugar pine plank, 7.5" x 12", natural varnish
DESCRIPTION: As I was beginning my painting on Saturday night of the Easter weekend, my daughter, Alicia McDonald, came home and was watching me. I shared with her that I felt strongly that she should participate in the spirit of the weekend by painting the anguish of Mary "the human mother" as her perfect child was being crucified.

She granted my wish by painting this retablo. The anguish Alicia captured on Mary's face is almost too much to live with. This retablo reeks of death and anguish. Note the black tears and the sword of sorrows in the top arch. Jesus' blood even drips down onto his mother as she weeps. There are no halos, however, the backdrop is yellow and orange. All of the colors are opaque and heavy. The cross is symbolized in all four corners.

Upon close examination, many varied entities can be seen in the backdrop. The face of a lamb can be found above Jesus' hand. A lion face is located in the lower right orange. Look closely for more.

To date, this is Alicia McDonald's only retablo painting.

At this point in time, the spiritual significance of my retablos was certainly making itself known. Everyone who was viewing them, and their individual characteristics was very curious and intrigued with what was developing on my living room wall.

Lady of Sorrow - Ritual/Celebration

PAINTED ORDER: 8
RETABLO: Reredo: Michael the Archangel - Reframe/Traditional
INSPIRATION: To paint a reredo of my family members
MEDIUM: Natural pigment, watercolors, rabbit skin glue gesso, sugar pine board, 7.25" x 9.25", natural varnish
DESCRIPTION: This was the first retablo I painted in my family reredos (grouped retablos.) It was also my first reredo. I discussed this process in more detail in My Retablo Awakening.

I had decided to represent my four family members with traditional saints that I felt were similar in attributes and symbols. This was also the first retablo painted in that frame of mind.

I chose Michael the Archangel to represent my father, John Carl Dougan, Sr., who had died from celiac sprue in 1959, at the age of 34. He was full-blood Irish from Pittsburgh. My Daddy was very protective of his family and no one ever challenged that stance. He definitely was my protector, my guardian angel, my friend, my Daddy. He called me Nini, which means "Daddy's little girl."

This retablo was easy to paint.

Reredo: Michael the Archangel - Reframe/Traditional

PAINTED ORDER: 9
RETABLO: Reredo: Our Lady of Sorrows - Reframe/Traditional
INSPIRATION: To paint a reredo of my family members
MEDIUM: Natural pigment, watercolors, rabbit skin glue gesso, sugar pine board, 7.25" x 9.25", natural varnish
DESCRIPTION: This was the second retablo I painted in my family reredo series and it came with more decision and thought than did the one of Daddy.

I'm not truly sure of the many subconscious reasons I chose Our lady of Sorrows to represent my Mother, Cora Juanita Dunlap Dougan. As I stated in My Retablo Awakening, my reframing process involved examining these individuals from their minds and hearts, from those of their best friends, and strangers. With that, I always saw great sorrow, fear and anxiety around my Mother. My Mother had a lot of hurt and emotions around her childhood and that shrouded her entire life. Her life seemed to me to have a lot of death and grief in it, including two husbands before she was 50. She always anticipated the pain of the negative and prepared herself for it.

I am aware that if she had ever read this, she would have disagreed and probably found more sorrow in my perception. Having examined this prior to materializing this retablo and rhetoric, I still feel strong about my choice here. I mean only to capture the reframing of my perception in this reredos. Strangers, and relatives who were held at bay by her, would have described her as an intelligent comic. I was not held at bay and I only saw the sad and fearful aloneness.

Reredo: Our Lady of Sorrows - Reframe/Traditional

PAINTED ORDER: 10
RETABLO: Reredo: St. Francis
INSPIRATION: To paint a reredo of my family members
MEDIUM: Natural pigment, watercolors, rabbit skin glue gesso, sugar pine board, 7.25" x 9.25", natural varnish
DESCRIPTION: This was the third retablo I painted in my family reredo series. The portrayal of St. Francis as my older brother, John Carl Dougan, Jr., was a relatively easy choice.

John is a noted author and a very articulate speaker. His passion as an adolescent was the breeding and training of his award-winning pigeon flock. John is also very conscious of environmental balances, and is an avid Biblical scholar. John is an internationally acclaimed author on the subject of Ruger guns, which could be framed as a duality.

Reredo: St. Francis

PAINTED ORDER: 11
RETABLO: Reredo: St. Christopher
INSPIRATION: To paint a reredo of my family members
MEDIUM: Natural pigment, watercolors, dirt, rabbit skin glue gesso, sugar pine board, 7.25" x 9.25", natural varnish
DESCRIPTION: This was the fourth and most difficult retablo I painted in my family reredo series. I really had to process a lot of layers of garbage to arrive at a simple process of reframing my younger brother, Michael Stanton Dougan. We have spent our lives viewing and experiencing the same scenarios from extremely different emotional perspectives. I am always shocked and amazed at how he has registered the same experiences that I have and the distrust and paranoia he has around me.

Therefore, I had to establish a different dimension from which to view my younger brother, Michael. I chose to examine his attributes through the eyes of his friends, spouse, children, strangers, and, as I perceived, his own point of view.

Mike is a tall, well-built man, as St. Christopher was. He has taken numerous strangers into the shelter of his home, including several foreign exchange students. Mike has an extraordinary energy level and is a very hard worker. He has always been a good and creative provider for his wife and their three children. I feel confident that there have been many times that Mike felt he carried the weight of the world on his shoulders, as did St. Christopher, the saint of travelers. As I look back on our childhood, the playful times that I remember were in the swimming pool, where Mike could sit crisscross-applesauce on the bottom of the pool. I couldn't even kick my way to the bottom of the pool, and he couldn't float. He loves to be in the water.

St. Christopher was a giant who pushed and pulled ferry boats filled with travelers across the river. One day a child asked St. Christopher to carry him to the other side of the river. By the time they reached the other shore, St. Christopher could hardly keep from collapsing into the water of the river. As the child climbed down from St. Christopher's shoulder, onto the shore, he said, "I am the Christ child, and you just carried the weight of the world."

Though I was finally able to effectively reframe my younger brother as a santos, I realize that reframing my perspective did not impact how he might still perceive me.

Reredo: St. Christopher

PAINTED ORDER: 12
RETABLO: Littleton's Sorrow - Event
INSPIRATION: Children Killing Children in Littleton, Colorado
MEDIUM: Water color on paper, 9" x 12"
DESCRIPTION: On April 20, 1999, two students embarked on a shooting rampage at Columbine High School, in Littleton, Colorado, killing 13 students, 1 teacher, and wounding 25 other students before committing suicide. This event rocketed America into an escaladed examination of the real lives of her children.

Wikepedia sums it up as follows: "The massacre provoked debate regarding gun control laws, the availability of firearms in the United States, and gun violence involving youths. Much discussion also centered on the nature of high school cliques, subcultures and bullying, as well as the role of violent movies and video games in American society. The shooting also resulted in an increased emphasis on school security, and a moral panic aimed at goth culture, social pariahs, the gun culture, the use of pharmaceutical anti-depressants by teenagers, music, and teenage internet use."

My heart joined the parental hearts of America in the realization that there are many cells within the dimensions of our youth that are in fact ticking time bombs which society and parents have chosen to ignor and deny. It took the drama and loss of this event to yank heads out of the sand and acknowledge that the societal problems even exist.

America is represented by the Virgin Mother, or Our Lady of Sorrows. Perhaps I should have depicted a gun as opposed to the dagger. However, it is the piercing, cutting of the very heart that I sought.

Littleton's Sorrow - Event

PAINTED ORDER: 13
RETABLO: Virgin of Guadalupe - Traditional Santos
INSPIRATION: She is the favored Virgin in New Mexico and I wanted to spend time with Her.
MEDIUM: Water color on paper, 7" x 10.5"
DESCRIPTION: The Virgin of Guadalupe is the obvious favorite saint in New Mexico. There are pieces of art, tattoos, clothing, and statues of her image all over the Southwest and Mexico. She is the only brown-skinned Catholic virgin santos.

I very much wanted to spend time getting to know her story and her image and to try my hand at capturing her essence. This retablo required more of my attention than usual, however, I am still very pleased with the resulting face and essence. She is one of my favorites.

Virgin of Guadalupe - Traditional Santos

PAINTED ORDER: 14
RETABLO: St. Georgia – Living Saint
INSPIRATION: Georgia O'Keefe, artist
MEDIUM: Natural pigment, water colors, rabbit skin glue gesso, poplar plank, 8.25" x 10.5", acrylic varnish
DESCRIPTION: Georgia O'Keefe is one of the most celebrated and acclaimed artist in the Southwest regions of America. Her story is powerful, and her work reflects the emotions of her life story. She traveled the United States, but was a loner who favored the solace and beauty of the Southwest. The latter part of her life was spent at Ghost Ranch, her home at Taos, New Mexico, where she painted the desert landscapes, sunsets, flowers and sun-bleached animal bones.

As a young woman, Georgia was a very successful model. She was known to be very sensuous and had to fight that reputation when she began to express her emotions through her paintings. She would often say that no matter what she painted, it would be interpreted a "sexual". With every year of her life, she became more reclusive.

Georgia is so beloved in the Southwest, that images of her work can be found for sale in most retail settings, and in most homes. She died at the age of 98, March 6, 1986.

I chose to parallel Georgia with St. Paul whose symbols are an ox and the tools of an artist. He is the saint of artists. Very interesting similarities, especially when you consider that Georgia put ox or cow bones in most all of her late pieces.

St. Georgia – Living Saint

PAINTED ORDER: 15
RETABLO: Goddess of Willendorf - Guru
INSPIRATION: She's the oldest Goddess
MEDIUM: Water color, dirt, paper 8" x 10"
DESCRIPTION: The 11.1 centimeter tall, limestone Goddess of Willendorf, or Venus of Willendorf, or Earth Goddess was discovered in 1908 outside Willendorf, Austria. She has been dated at 24,000 BCE.

Christopher Witcombe states that *"Her great age and pronounced female forms quickly established the Venus of Willendorf as an icon of prehistoric art. She was soon included in introductory art history textbooks where she quickly displaced other previously used examples of Paleolithic art. Being both female and nude, she fitted perfectly into the patriarchal construction of the history of art. As the earliest known representation, she became the "first woman", acquiring a sort of Ur-Eve identity that focused suitably, from a patriarchal point of view, on the fascinating reality of the female body."*

Being a full-figured woman myself, and very intrigued with the attention given to goddesses, both in art and jewelry, I felt that the Goddess of Willendorf stands as the female icon and should be included in this study.

Goddess of Willendorf - Guru

PAINTED ORDER: 16
RETABLO: Dr. Ernest Holmes – Guru – Spiritual Mentor
INSPIRATION: Spiritual leader and author
MEDIUM: Water color, gesso, poplar plank 8" x 12"
DESCRIPTION: Dr. Ernest Holmes is the author of Science of Mind and the founder of the Church of Religious Science, which is nationally undergoing a name change to Center for Spiritual Living. Among its original followers were Einstein, Emerson, Hopkins, and Troward. He used religion, physics, philosophy, and theology to study the universe and the religious beliefs of people around the globe. He used scientific rationalization, logic, deductive, and inductive thinking to interpret the major scriptural writings that men hold sacred. He teaches oneness and unity, which is represented in the yellow symbol above Dr. Holmes in the retablo.

It is because of the 20 years that I have studied these metaphysical teachings that I was able to lunge forward, snapping an arrow in two with the base of my throat, and to walk on fire at the Native American Indian Culture Center in Albquerque, New Mexico, October 2006.

The following quote is written on the back of the original retablo: "I am the medium through which God chooses to experience Life."

Dr. Ernest Holmes – Guru – Spiritual Mentor

PAINTED ORDER: 17
RETABLO: St. Evie - Living Saint
INSPIRATION: Evalu Gillett Howard
MEDIUM: Natural pigment water colors, rabbit skin glue gesso, sugar pine plank 8.25" x 10.75"
DESCRIPTION: My long time friend, Evalu, and I used to work in the same mall in Amarillo, Texas. I was in cosmetics at Dillards; she managed Zales. We always took our breaks and meals together so we could discuss Life's curves and giggles. Most of our time, however, was spent in the discussion of male/female relationships, a topic we managed to dissect ten thousand directions.

As time moved on, so did we. In fact, we actually lost contact for about five years. Then the Universe brought us back together, with our vow to never lose contact again. I have never lost my desire to buy a cup of coffee with a Bavarian pretzel and cheese, and sit down to discuss concerns of the heart with Evie. Even through the years of separation, I would go there in my mind, and refer to our many resolves. I always found solace there.

In May of 1999, I had emerged myself into my retablo paintings on several different dimensions and with diversified focus. So, when I found myself on the verge of a relationship with some extraordinary circumstances surrounding it, I felt an intense desperation to sit down with coffee, pretzel, cheese and Evie. But, Evie was not accessible that week and I knew I must find another tool to serve me. So, I decided to spend the entire night painting St. Evie as I talked my way through the mental dissections.

I had just entered my period of using traditional saints to parallel my personal living saints and gurus. (You can read more about that dialog in the first chapters of this book.) It was easy to choose St. Cecilia to depict Evie. St. Cecilia is the saint of poets and musicians and is credited for inventing the organ. St. Cecilia is always very regal, captivating and lovely. Evie is all of that and more.

I always smile, giggle, and reminisce when my eyes gaze on St. Evie. For many reasons, she is one of my cherished retablos.

St. Evie - Living Saint

PAINTED ORDER: 18
RETABLO: Jesus' Bleeding Heart - Traditional Santo
INSPIRATION: My desire to paint Jesus
MEDIUM: Natural pigment, water colors, rabbit skin glue gesso, poplar plank, 8" x 12"
DESCRIPTION: This retablo was my first attempt at coming up with my own personal design for Jesus as a santo. I wanted to keep it simple and not stray from the primitive look of vintage retablos. I was pleased with my first attempt. So much so that I again used the same image to construct #24, except that I also wanted to experiment with raised gesso to create a relief effect.

Jesus' Bleeding Heart - Traditional Santo

PAINTED ORDER: 19
RETABLO: Michael the Archangel - Traditional
INSPIRATION: Desire to paint Michael with black hair
MEDIUM: Natural pigment, water colors, rabbit skin glue gesso, poplar plank, 8" x 12"
DESCRIPTION: I have a small statue of Michael the Archangel that was made in Italy. It is one of my favorite things, and has been in my life for many years. I looked at that statue in order to draw Michael. It is the same basic design I used for #8 in my family reredo.

Every time I looked at the reredo, I wanted to change some of the colors, especially Michael's hair color. Often Michael is portrayed as having blonde hair, so I had gone along with that in the reredo. However, my Daddy had black hair and all warriors in my mind have black hair. In addition, I resonate with him, and felt compelled to paint a second Michael. I also added the additional symbol of the scale right after the word Michael on the border. This is my favorite Michael.

Michael the Archangel - Traditional

PAINTED ORDER: 20
RETABLO: St. Alicia - Living Saint
INSPIRATION: Alicia's Birthday
MEDIUM: Watercolor, rabbit skin glue gesso, poplar plank 8" x 12"
DESCRIPTION: I was standing in line at the post office, when I noticed the most beautiful new stamp. It was of a ballerina with a long, white tutu on. She was standing on one leg, arching far backward, with her other leg stretched up behind her. The ballerina was a gorgeous blonde and she looked just like my oldest daughter, Alicia. It was one of the most beautiful photographs that I've ever seen. The flow of the body and the lightness of the ballerina was breath-taking.

Since Alicia loves fairies and sunflowers. I painted her as a fairy floating on the top of a bubble past a giant sunflower, with the breeze flowing over her body and wings. Alicia's body is in the same pose as the ballerina. Alicia likes to wear scarves around her delicate neck, so I added that detail.

The back of the retablo reads:
Saint Alicia: The saint of unconditional love and keeper of friendships.

She darts from life to life weaving an invisible web of golden threads that connect souls for eternity. She enters with a smile and sprinkles souls with magic bubbles of baby giggles as she flits off again.

It's easy to tell where she is present because there will be smiles, giggles, or bubbles.

Her size and visibility change as needed, however, Saint Alicia is of the Fairy specie when in true form, and can always be identified by the fairy markings on her slender back and the calf of her leg.

Happy 21st Birthday!
I love you, Mom
6-18-99

St. Alicia - Living Saint

PAINTED ORDER: 21
RETABLO: Moses - Traditional
INSPIRATION: Time Magazine cover, 1998
MEDIUM: Watercolor, rabbit skin glue gesso, wood, 8" x 12"
DESCRIPTION: A retablo collection would not be complete without Moses. That, coupled with my finding the December 14, 1998, issue of Time magazine in the doctor's office, inspired this retablo. The feature story of that issue was "Who Was Moses?" The cover was a very old depiction of Moses holding the Ten Commandments. It was painted on cracked board, in almost a Byzantine style. The lines are very simple and patterned. Very stylized. I could hardly wait to get home to study and learn from this masterpiece. I not only honor Moses, but the artist who excited me to copy his work.

Moses - Traditional

PAINTED ORDER: 22
RETABLO: Self Portrait – Self
INSPIRATION: Need to try to align my essence with a saint
MEDIUM: Acrylic on canvas, 20" x 24"
DESCRIPTION: Since one facet of my workshop is to paint one's self as a saint, I had to attempt to find myself in the retablo setting. Based on the saints I knew of, I was always, and still am, intrigued with Mary Madeline. So, I added southwest jewelry and white hair and painted myself into the retablo. However, even today, I don't resonate with this depiction. I am still caught in the quandary of what my attributes are and which saint I parallel. The nuns next door, some 9 years later, tell me St. Elizabeth. We'll see. I'm thinking Mother Teresa of Calcutta.

Not shown in this scan of the painting is a heart with a sword piercing it. It is laying on the brown adobe wall to the left side of the painting. She is looking down at it.

Self Portrait – Self

PAINTED ORDER: 23
RETABLO: C of Hearts - Relationship
INSPIRATION: Ended Relationship
MEDIUM: Watercolor on paper, 9" x 12"
DESCRIPTION: Carlos was from Belize. He grew up in the rain forest of Central America and was an accomplished martial artist, athlete, and fugitive detective. He was 5'7", 147 pounds of energy, wisdom, and fascination. He could move so quickly that his hand would be waiting for the fly when it arrived. His tales of living among the animals, developing the senses of his life energy, seeing auras, using his thoughts to create his illusions, and his international travels always kept me spell bound. He was like finding Tarzan in the middle of Albuquerque. At the age of 58, he was a legend among one thousand police officers. There was no doubt. His Latin accent was music to my ears, as was his soft laughter.

Though we didn't get much physical time together in the year that we dated, I learned a great deal from Carlos. I learned to live in the moment. To be present now, for one or the other of us may die before we are together again. Nothing is permanent, so spend your time in love not fear, and cherish each other. Really cherish. He also made the statement that we always leave part of ourself behind in exchange for part of the other person in each encounter.

As I continued to paint retablos, sometimes night and day, I desired to honor our relationship. To capture the essence of the goodness and the oneness that I had experienced when I was with Carlos. So I used playing cards and symbols of us to create the C of Hearts. I intertwined us and our worlds and painted it for my heart to see and remember our beautiful time together in this life.

C of Hearts - Relationship

PAINTED ORDER: 24
RETABLO: Jesus' Bleeding Heart - Traditional
INSPIRATION: To experiment with gesso
MEDIUM: Watercolor, raised gesso, wood, 8" x 12"
DESCRIPTION: This retablo is the same as #18 except that I used layers of gesso to raise details of the painting, creating a relief technique. The colors are brighter in this retablo than #18. The details that are raised are the heart, face, and border. The face is raised in such a manner that the nose is the highest point, and it graduates down to the ears.

I was very pleased with the resulting retablo, especially the brighter pigments. However, the face and border has started to crack after 9 years, which is a plus and a minus. It does give it a vintage look.

Jesus' Bleeding Heart - Traditional

PAINTED ORDER: 25
RETABLO: Two Angels – Living Saints
INSPIRATION: My Two Granddaughters
MEDIUM: Acrylic on canvas, 9" x 12"
DESCRIPTION: Falicia asked me to paint a picture of her and Brittney. They were 7 and 4, respectively. As I mentioned, I had never painted a portrait of anyone, especially with acrylic, so, this was a real challenge. Keep in mind that I had not entered college in pursuit of an art degree yet.

At the age of seven, Falicia's front teeth hadn't grown back in, and her eyes were still crossed. Her self esteem was bruised and she needed to see herself calm, angelic, and pretty. She wanted her short hair to be long and shiny, so, I painted the girls older and as angels with long hair. I remember her asking me if I really thought she would grow up and be that pretty. To this day, this painting hangs in Falicia's bedroom. I expect that it always will.

Two Angels – Living Saints

PAINTED ORDER: 26
RETABLO: Jesus' Thorns - Traditional
INSPIRATION: Thorns
MEDIUM: Acrylic on wood plank, 7" x 10.5"
DESCRIPTION: I saw a photograph of a painting of Jesus in a magazine. The thorn crown that was on Jesus' head was huge, and the thorns were fat and green. That's all I remembered about the picture. The thorns. I spent a lot of time thinking about the thorns and wondering if they were in fact that big. And green.

I sat down to draw Jesus in such a fashion as to capture the anguish and exhaustion with the simplest of lines. And, of course, the thorns had to be substantial. I also was curious about how much impact on the emotions the type of medium would have. So, I painted the drawing in acrylic, and watercolor #27. I feel that both of these retablos are quite effective, especially in the fact that there is no actual cross in the painting design.

PAINTED ORDER: 27
RETABLO: Jesus' Thorns, watercolor - Traditional
INSPIRATION: Thorns
MEDIUM: Watercolor, gesso, wood, 7" x 12"
DESCRIPTION: This is the same description as #26, except that it is painted in water color and is a different shape. Since the wood plank is longer, I positioned Jesus at the bottom in order to give the perception of weight on his shoulders. Which of the two paintings has greater emotional impact?

PAINTED ORDER: 28
RETABLO: Stand Like Mountain, Move Like Water – Ritual/ Celebration
INSPIRATION: The story
MEDIUM: Watercolor and dirt on wood, 7.25" x 12"
DESCRIPTION: A guitar-wielding troubadour touched my heart with a song he wrote about an 85 year-old Chinese lady who had been kept a political prisoner in absolute dark solitude for seven years. The troubadour first told us of her strength, her peace, her light, her story, their friendship. When he asked her how she maintained her strength and survived it all, she answered him, "You must stand like a mountain, yet move like the water."

The song spoke of her hope that somehow her light shone beyond the darkness and the seeds of her strength and hope would find root and grow. I painted this retablo on the Fourth of July in celebration of the strength of this woman's life and in honor of the troubadour's heart.

Jesus' Thorns - Traditional

Jesus' Thorns, watercolor - Traditional

Stand Like Mountain, Move Like Water – Ritual/Celebration

PAINTED ORDER: 29
RETABLO: Spirit Weaver - Third Party Channel
INSPIRATION: Patron Request; Gorman art style
MEDIUM: Acrylic on wood, 9" x 12" beveled oval
DESCRIPTION: On the morning of Mothers' Day, 1999, my girls and myself arrived at the home of my friend Trish and her daughter Kirstin. We were to travel together to Taos, New Mexico, on a rock-hounding venture.

Trish first brought me to her kitchen where she had set out six tiny baskets. She instructed me to chose one for my Mother's Day gift. She explained how her friend Kim makes her living weaving these tiny baskets from ponderosa pine needles, palm leaves, feathers and beads. She told me how Kim prays and blesses each inspired basket throughout the process of weaving and upon completion. I was very touched by Kim's life story and by the gift.

While we were searching the forest for our "star fairy" stones, we stopped and gathered pinion sap nodules for my varnish and a trash bag of ponderosa pine needles to send to Kim in Alaska, where pine trees don't grow. Again, as I thanked the trees for the pine needles I was gathering for this unique weaver, I thought how odd that she makes her living from these tiny baskets and yet she lives in an area so far away from pine trees. I was amazed at how dependent she is on friends to ship the needles to her often enough to weave while they are still green and malleable. My mind moved to the realization that in a couple of days these very needles that I held in my hands would be the medium through which Kim's hands would weave healings. I was awestruck.

At this time, I was only about eight retablos into my process and I had brought color copies of them to show Trish. She really studied them and was able to instantly understand them, and to see the many varied images they contained. She even pointed out new images to me.

About five or six weeks later, Trish told me that she wanted to buy a retablo print for Kim whenever I got ready to release them. She told me how she had described the retablos to Kim and she wanted one. She had asked Kim which retablo she wanted, and Kim told her I would know which one to send. Again I was touched by this distant friend with whom I had become connected to through Trish. I looked at all of the retablos I had painted thus far and was not compelled to pick any of them for Kim. What I was inspired to do was to paint Kim's storyboard. I unveiled it at my party the following week, with Trish present. Trish held the retablo in her hands and asked about the heart in the tree trunk. I told her that I had not consciously thought about the heart. It was one of the first symbols I drew into the design. It is not something that I would ordinarily put into any of my art due to its overuse and novel connotations.

Trish continued on to tell me about the dream that Kim had shared with her during their last phone conversation. It was all about a pine tree with a heart in the trunk. Trish tells me that my spirit Weaver looks like Kim, except that Kim has short hair. Then, as we walk into my bedroom to look at a painting, Trish postures herself beside my bed and inquires as to why I chose my particular bedspread and linen set. I told her I had just bought it about 3 weeks prior, because I liked the magic magenta and the stained glass images. She then says, "Kim has the same one." Perhaps I was in her room when she dreamed the tree with a heart, which was about the same time I purchased the linens. Funny, until the moment of this writing, I had assumed that she had come to me. Curious.

Spirit Weaver - Third Party Channel

PAINTED ORDER: 30
RETABLO: St. Francis - Traditional
INSPIRATION: Garden statue of St. Francis
MEDIUM: Acrylic on Canvas, 10" x 20"
DESCRIPTION: Leafing through a mail order catalog, I found a wonderful garden statue of St. Francis. I loved it so much that I decided to use it as my inspiration to paint a more simplified version of St. Francis than the one I used in the family reredo. I chose acrylic on canvas because I was wanting to further experiment with the medium, and I wanted to create energy in the paint itself. The lines of his face are so simple and loving that the painting easily captures the heart of the viewer.

PAINTED ORDER: 31
RETABLO: Poseidon – Living Saint
INSPIRATION: Nick Bronson
MEDIUM: Watercolor, dirt, rabbit skin glue gesso, wood, 8.5" x 12"
DESCRIPTION: Poseidon was painted as a tribute to my friend, Nick Bronson, who is getting his degree in marine biology in Alaska. He is an avid fisherman, reader, and scholar. His mind is a steel trap and worthy of guarding the history of the universe. His quotations are infinite and wise. His journey the first half of his life was quite stormy; the second half brings the gifts and manifestations of wisdom.

The retablo has a stone wall in the background and a Greek column representing Atlantis. The top border design represents the sunrises that Nick so loves and photographs. The crown symbolizes that he realizes the Christ in himself and others. The three scrolls have letters on them representing N/Nick, A/Atlantis, and L/Life; three subjects that Nick examines continually. The column provides a place for Poseidon to put items he is contemplating; "G" for God, and seahorses for possible gifts to man, as the history goes. The yellow archway serves as a halo and the extended yellow beneath his left arm forms an arrow representative of Poseidon's brother Zeus. Poseidon is wisdom and strength.

Nick has always inspired me to continue seeking and he is truly proof of man's ability to change. He is one of the greatest souls I've ever known. Nick gave me the quote written on the back of the original retablo:

"A smooth sea never a wise mariner made." - unknown

St. Francis - Traditional

Poseidon – Living Saint

PAINTED ORDER: 32
RETABLO: Pieta – Reframe
INSPIRATION: National Pieta Art Exhibit in Santa Fe
MEDIUM: Watercolor, rabbit skin glue gesso, wood, 7" x 11"
DESCRIPTION: For our mother and daughter outing, Alicia and I drove to Santa Fe, New Mexico, to eat lunch and attend a national art exhibit entitled "Pieta." The exhibit was in the Santuario de Virgin Guadalupe, an old adobe mission. Pieta is a Greek word that refers to a mother and her dead son. It is most often used to refer to Mother Mary holding Jesus at the foot of the cross.

The show contained roughly one hundred works of art from across America. The ones that I recall most vividly were painted by nuns. One in particular was of a nun holding a teen-aged boy who had been shot in a gang war. This wonderful, memorable show was indeed very emotionally packed. The styles varied from traditional retablo watercolors to gold leaf embellished Byzantine oils. From primitive to old masters.

I so resonated with the essence of the show and the fact that my own son's life had been destroyed by drugs, mental illness, alcohol, and violence. With that, I painted myself and my son, William Paul Burgess, on the stage of life, but his wounds are from needles, which are even part of the backdrop design. I was so caught up in the process of painting this retablo that I didn't realize for months that I had painted his feet reversed. The distortion, however, adds to the effectiveness of the piece of art as a retablo. It creates a stress for the viewer.

Pieta – Reframe

PAINTED ORDER: 33
RETABLO: Jesus, Celtic - Traditional
INSPIRATION: Pieta Exhibit
MEDIUM: Watercolor, gold leaf, rabbit skin glue gesso, wood, 9" x 14"
DESCRIPTION: The ad in the newspaper for the Pieta art exhibit I described in #31 had a photograph of Jesus, designed in a Celtic style. The oil painting was very large and magnificent. Having had a pedigree Irish father, I'm always intrigued with Celtic. In addition, I wanted to use gold leaf in my retablos. Having studied with Glenda Green, the artist who paints historically correct portraits of famous people, I gave Jesus green eyes and medium brown hair, as she said he would have had based on demographics. I am fond of the symmetric designs of this retablo.

In the process of painting this piece, I was very aware of the scripture that I quoted on the back. I was working on my state of expectation and gratitude at the time. Well, I still am.

The back of the retablo reads: Luke 12:32 "Fear not, little flock, for it is your Father's good pleasure to give you the kingdom."
"Love is who you are." - Glenda Green's Interview with Jesus

Jesus, Celtic - Traditional

PAINTED ORDER: 34
RETABLO: Emerson - Guru
INSPIRATION: His writings
MEDIUM: Watercolor on wood, 9" x 14"
DESCRIPTION: Ralph Waldo Emerson was a brilliant writer. He studied quantum physics and metaphysics. His books and lectures are part of my spiritual teachings. I have taken accredited classes that were built around the content of his work. He encourages one to listen to the Self within.

The style of this retablo is almost too life-like. I think a more primitive likeness might have been better, however, some of the vintage retablos are equally life like in their likeness.

The back of the retablo reads:
"A man should learn to detect and watch that gleam of light which flashes across his mind from within, more than the luster of the firmament of bards and sages."
- Ralph Waldo Emerson

Emerson - Guru

PAINTED ORDER: 35
RETABLO: Hopkins - Guru
INSPIRATION: Her writings
MEDIUM: Watercolor on wood, 8" x 12"
DESCRIPTION: Emma Curtis Hopkins was a brilliant writer and teacher. She studied and taught quantum physics and metaphysics. Her books are part of my spiritual teachings. I have taken accredited classes that were built around the content of her work. Her focus seemed, to me, to be on effective prayer. She was so mystic, so powerful.

The style of this retablo, also, is almost too life-like. I think that a more primitive likeness might have been better, however, some of the vintage retablos are equally life like in their likeness. However, the largeness and distortion of her eyes effectively speaks of her mysticism.

Written on the back:
"I acknowledge the presence of anxiety and fear regarding my intentions. However, anxiety and fear have no power. The only power is Good. My Good is my God. My God is my Good. Therefore, I lovingly release anything that stands between me and my greatest Good. And so it is." --- Hopkins

Hopkins - Guru

PAINTED ORDER: 36
RETABLO: Grace - Reframe
INSPIRATION: Sermon on Judas
MEDIUM: Watercolor, metallic, rabbit skin glue gesso, wood , 9" x 11"
DESCRIPTION: When sermons are given on Judas, he is almost always painted as an evil person who somehow slipped into Jesus' closely-knit followers. I had always questioned why Jesus would have allowed that. Why would any of the apostles allowed it. They would not have afforded to take the risks of a traitor among them. Therefore, when a guest preacher painted Judas so differently, I had to celebrate this truth in a retablo.

Judas and Jesus were best of friends as children. Judas was from a very wealthy family, and he lacked for nothing. He loved Jesus very much and Jesus loved him. Judas believed Jesus' teachings so much that he wanted the world to know. He couldn't understand why Jesus was content to walk about the country side and sea shores teaching the small crowds when he could be teaching countries. Judas did not need anyone's money. He was wealthy. He had thought that if he led the soldiers to Jesus, that Jesus would stand up to them and work miracles in such a way that no one could deny who he was and then Jesus' ministry and teachings would be acclaimed everywhere. Judas thought he was setting the stage for Jesus to be revered and worshipped as he himself did. He was calling attention to Jesus, not to get him crucified, but to announce Him as the Son of God. When his actions caused the abuse and crucifixion of Jesus, Judas' heart was broken and he could not stand to live with the agony of what he had done, so he leaped to his death.

Jesus, of course, knew the necessary events of his life. He knew how the pieces had to fit together. This retablo is about Jesus' love and understanding for Judas. I call it Grace. I understand Grace to be the ever-present Love of God without conditions. God is Love. Love is all there is; the rest we made up.

I used the circle of oneness and stylized the Science of Mind "V" symbol to capture the omnipresence, omnipotence, and omniscience of God's Love.

Grace - Reframe

PAINTED ORDER: 37
RETABLO: Innocence
INSPIRATION: A child's story
MEDIUM: Watercolor, rabbit skin glue gesso, wood
DESCRIPTION: It was Christmas, and the Sunday School teacher had asked the children to draw the manger where the baby Jesus was born. After everyone finished their drawing, the teacher asked them to each show the class. As the teacher studied the drawing that little Johnny had done, she pointed to the circle figure standing beside Mary and asked "Who is this, Johnny?" With a bit of puzzle and indignity, Johnny pointed to each of the three people in his drawing and replied "Why that's Round John Virgin, Mother, and child."

I love this story. It reminds me that Christmas is about children and life. It is when celebration and merriment should ring throughout. So, I seized the opportunity to paint a Christmas retablo that brings laughter to our home each year. It is naïve and simple. It is Christmas. I call it Inn-O-Cence. Enjoy.

Oh, the year that I printed Christmas cards of this image, I did send one to the president of the M & M candy company. I never heard back.

Innocence

PAINTED ORDER: 38
RETABLO: Carlos the Archangel - Living Saint
INSPIRATION: Carlos Garcia, of Belize
MEDIUM: Watercolor, rabbit skin glue gesso, wood, 7" x 18"
DESCRIPTION: Michael the Archangel is the saint of policemen and warriors. So, it was an easy choice to paint Carlos, the fugitive detective from Belize, as Michael. I had previously painted Carlos in my C of Hearts retablo. However, he had come back into my life for a brief time, and I wanted to revisit his essence in a single image. I was pleased in my ability to capture his facial likeness and the overall mood of the retablo.

Carlos had three sons. Two of them were executed by gangs and he continually worried about Carlos, Jr. Though Carlos had been given custody of the grandchildren who were orphaned, he had let an upper class white family adopt them so they would have a set of parents, money for ballet and college, and he would not have to worry about their fate if he should be shot down in action. He was still their grandfather and active in their life, however.

He was the primary care-giver of his aged mother and he was a very accomplished martial artist. He had a drum collection that contained hand-made drums from around the world and when he played, he would play for days, drumming with the heart beat. But it was rare that he had time for this passion. At the time I knew him, he was 58 years of age and he had been awarded the most physically fit police officer in a community of one thousand, without being graded on a curve. His energy, both physical and ethereally were amazing and intriguing. But the sadness of the loss of his sons and the ever-present death in his profession showed in his face. I knew him to be the ultimate warrior and care-giver, with one foot in each world at all times. Though he brought me many valuable lessons that I shall always speak of, the most valued was that now is all we really have. Savor it.

Carlos the Archangel - Living Saint

PAINTED ORDER: 39
RETABLO: St. Gary - Living Saint
INSPIRATION: Gary Kent McDonald
MEDIUM: Natural pigment, watercolor, rabbit skin glue gesso, plywood, 12" x 14"
DESCRIPTION: Gary Kent McDonald is my oldest daughter's father. He is an intelligent, gentle, well-read, educated man who has the gift of stepping outside himself and seeing both sides of a situation without being biased in his conclusions. He is steadfast and true to his beliefs and opinions. Though a sensitive man, he could and would even resist my attempts to personally sway him over to my side in a given scenario. His profession has always been as a commercial artist, however I have always thought he would make a superior judge. We were only married some seven years and we had one child together, Alicia. It became obvious that our marriage suffered from incompatibility and we went on to build separate lives. Gary stayed involved in Alicia's life and has always been a perfect Dad and granddad. He is a scholarly man of integrity.

I chose St. Jerome as the traditional saint to portray Gary. St. Jerome was a highly respected scholar whose symbols are books and a lion. The legend goes that St. Jerome was so fierce that few people dared to speak with him. One day a lion with a sticker in his paw, knocked on St. Jerome's door and St. Jerome gently removed the sticker and doctored the lion's paw. From then on the lion never left St. Jerome's side. The lion adds another dimension that speaks of Gary. Because of his love and understanding of animals, as a student, Gary worked in a veterinarian's office.

This retablo is the only one that I painted on plywood. Over the years the surface of the plywood and the gesso have cracked, giving it the same vintage look that the Time magazine photo of Moses reflected (see Moses retablo.) It does present a rather nice effect, however, the magenta prickly pear cactus pigment fades with time.

St. Gary - Living Saint

PAINTED ORDER: 40
RETABLO: St. Richard – Living Saint
INSPIRATION: Richard Foran
MEDIUM: Watercolor on wood, 8" x 11"
DESCRIPTION: St. Richard, Master Carpenter, was painted to honor my life-long platonic friend, Richard Foran. He and I met as co-workers and have remained close friends for nearly three decades, even as we have lived many states apart. We are both grandparents now.

Over the years, Richard has gifted me several handmade altar and jewelry boxes. Though his trade is not that of a carpenter, his passion as a master craftsman is very evident in his seamless work.

I created Richard's image without reference to any traditional santos. I depicted him as the queen's master carpenter, creating royal heirlooms. I drew him as the big man that he is. The box that he is shown to be constructing is the altar box that he built for me.

Written on the back:
"May you live a thousand years and I a thousand less one day that I may never know you passed away." - signed Richard

St. Richard – Living Saint

PAINTED ORDER: 41
RETABLO: St. Roy – Living Saint
INSPIRATION: "Uncle" Roy Dunlap
MEDIUM: Watercolor on poplar wood, absorbent gesso, 8" x 12"
DESCRIPTION: I purchased a two foot by eight inch panel of poplar wood from Lowe's yesterday. The young man who waited on me was kind enough to saw it in half so I would have two planks. This purchase would allow me to paint two retablos: myself and Roy. These two paintings will complete this book process.

When I look in my head and heart for the vision of Roy as a retablo, I see so much goodness that it is difficult to keep my design simple. In fact, I'm not sure that I can do that, because much of his appeal is that he is such a multi-tasker and relentless work horse, that to put him into an un-cluttered setting might do him an injustice. Obviously, I am typing the descriptions of both my self retablo and Roy's, as I brainstorm how the retablos must look. What are the attributes? What are the symbols?

Roy is a medical wonder. The Great Experiment. He is the saint of both doctors and patients. He is the bridge between them. He endures extreme and excessive pain so patients of the future can live. He sees the river between life and death and walks both shores simultaneously, to the degree that there is no division. Every millisecond is a contract he holds between God and the medical world. He agrees to participate for the good of humanity, even at great odds and costs to himself. The struggle has become monotonous and mundane to him after nearly two decades. He can be seen talking on the phone, texting, or answering email while vile procedures are being run on his physical body. His reframing is superior. He challenges both death and life and goes about his mission, his purpose, of serving the individuals who are incarcerated in America's prisons. He lobbies. He lectures. He monitors. He is their voice in the political forums across this country. But above all, he is "Uncle Roy," a very dear and true friend to thousands of inmates. He is steadfast in answering hundreds of personal letters in a day, in writing monthly newsletters, in providing resources to the inmates, in pursuit of changing lives through friendship and prison reform. These individuals are his therapy, his connection and continuation of life. They are truly the reason he gets up in the morning, and are in his thoughts as he sleeps.

So, I called Roy and told him I was about to design his retablo and I had questions. I asked him what his attributes are, his symbols, his colors, etc. And what he told me follows: I am about communicating. I am generous. I like to be in the back room doing the work. I don't need to be in the lime light. I like orange, not red. My sword is taller than I am, like Joshua in the Bible. I want wings like John Travolta in "Michael." I like cats, not dogs. Cows are cool, but pigs are anti-social and slobs. I have a tendancy to weigh everything and everyone, like Michael does with his scales. I always question, so I can go forward. My favorite garment is my soft, hooded monk robe. It's warm and cuddly. My birthday is December 17. I like books and lists. Wow, I thought to myself. And I added to the list that he cooks pumpkin pie for company, and to fill the air when things run awry or people need happy thoughts.

When I entered "saint of generosity" into the Google.com search engine field, it came up with the Bishop of Myra, who was canonized as St. Nicholas, aka Santa Claus. His symbol is a crest with 3 coins, which represent generosity. I sat back in my chair and laughed right out loud. Everything, right down to the smells of Christmas, fit Uncle Roy. Even a December birthday. So, here you have it.

St. Roy – Living Saint

PAINTED ORDER: 42
EX VOTO: St. Carol - Self
INSPIRATION: Mother Teresa of Calcutta
MEDIUM: Watercolor on poplar wood, absorbent gesso, 8" x 12"
DESCRIPTION: It's been nine years since I painted my first retablo. And here I am, completing this book manuscript for publication. In my heart of hearts, I know that the book is not complete until I am complete in the painting of myself as an image that I resonate with. Therefore, I have spent weeks visiting that realization.

I was next door at the nuns' house last week, telling them about my latest trip into one of the Ohio prisons, when one of them actually asked which saint I personally identified with. I said "I don't know. I've never come up with that answer." She smiled at me and said, "I think St. Elizabeth. She took care of the needy." As a result, I came home and searched the internet for descriptions. After a couple of hours of reading about all of the different St. Elizabeths, I did not feel that she was the answer.

Finally, about a week later, I received a letter from an inmate, asking about my request for a painting of Mother Teresa. In fact, I have been asking for renderings or paintings of Mother Teresa for about two years now, and I still don't have one, which is unusual. I've purchased and read about ten books written about her life, and about Mother Antonia, The Prison Angel, who spent their life in service under extreme circumstances, such as going into prisons.

There is a particular photo of Mother Teresa walking past an adobe jail house window in India. That is the picture that calls to me. I am also feeling compelled to go beyond the traditional retablo style to that of an ex voto, which is more of a storyboard with text, and includes an inset of the saint that the painter credits with the miracle or the divinity of the storyboard. It was with the reading of this letter that the vision came to me to quit asking artists to paint Mother Teresa, whom I speak of a great deal, and to paint my self portrait as an ex voto with Mother Teresa inserted above the scene of myself and prison. As I began to draw, my inner self began to draw me inside the prison, as opposed to walking past the outside window. Being able to add the text that I so often quote makes this retablo image one that I personally resonate with.

Into my design, I included the muses depicted by drama masks, music symbols and art brushes in my hand, and a group of dancing signs that came to me. I included the icon of books for education, a green vine for life and connectedness, and roses and hearts for love. I inserted a monkey for my animal guide. Instead of a traditional halo or arch, I chose to represent radiance with yellow bars and lines of perspective, along with magenta stars of energy and spirituality in the cells and around both me and Mother Teresa. I chose purple as my main color, and its complementary color of yellow to create movement. And finally, I boldly used my name in the title, not a metaphor.

St. Carol - Self

RABBIT SKIN GLUE GESSO RECIPE

78 grams of rabbit skin glue granules or powder
1 quart water
Mix together and soak overnight.
Heat on low heat in a ceramic or stainless steel pot until all particles are dissolved.
A double boiler prevents overheating.
Brush a thin coat of warm glue onto your prepared boards.
Pour a cup of warm glue into a one quart yogurt carton.
Sift 1/2 to 3/4 lb. of marble dust (gypsum, limestone, or whiting - available in art supply stores) into the warm glue until the glue is saturated.

Keeping the gesso warm in a pan of warm water, coat the boards, let dry, and coat again if needed.

I recently used acrylic gesso [note: it must be absorbent gesso] just to try it, and it worked with watercolor. I had tried it years ago with no luck, with bad results. Maybe this was a different brand of gesso. But if you use acrylic gesso, you can't use alcohol based varnish, which is what I use on my traditional retablos.

PINION SAP NODULE VARNISH RECIPE

Fill a quart jar half full of sap nodules from pinion trees. The nodules are the external sap lumps that the tree has secreted in order to close a wound. Fill the jar with 100 proof Everclear alcohol and let it set for about two weeks before using it. You can leave the sap in the jar and gently stir before using, or you may choose to pour the liquid through cheese cloth after a month and throw away the fiber. The liquid is the natural varnish for coating your retablos. It also makes them smell good. After the varnish has dried, you can rub a square of beeswax onto the surface to further seal and to add a nice feel to the retablo surface.

I am one cell in the body of God. Basically, there can be no real enmity between me and any other cell. There can be no angry competition between us, because each of us is always working for the other, consciously or unconsciously.

I refuse to misunderstand others, and I refuse to be misunderstood. I believe that to know all is to forgive all. Therefore, I know that what appears to be hostile looks, words, or actions are only the effort of another to be secure within himself.

I carry the feeling of forgiveness toward anyone who has wronged me. I refuse to entertain suspicion toward those who have not wronged me. I cultivate the expectancy of good in all people, and I draw from them the same feelings. And so it is."

- author unknown

* * * * *

Affect is the millisecond that you realize that you were made by, for, and out of God and you should be living your life on a different dimension.

- author unknown

36566191R00058

Made in the USA
Charleston, SC
08 December 2014